Christian First-Aid Kit

How to Respond in a Crisis

Andrew Wommack

Published in partnership between Andrew Wommack Ministries and Harrison House Publishers.

 Woodland Park, CO 80863 – Shippensburg, PA 17257

ISBN 13 TP: 978-1-59548-707-0

For Worldwide Distribution, Printed in the USA

1 2 3 4 5 6 / 27 26 25 24

Contents

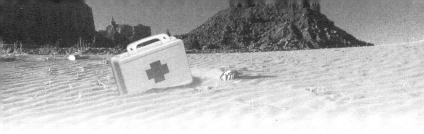

Introduction

Do you find yourself in a crisis situation? Do you feel like you are really between a rock and a hard place? Are you facing problems that, in your mind, seem insurmountable?

When you're facing a crisis, remember what Jesus said to His disciples the night before His crucifixion: "*Let not your heart be troubled*" (John 14:1). You may be thinking, *But you just don't know what I'm going through!* Maybe I don't, and I'm not trying to dismiss your situation, but what you are going through is nothing like what Jesus' disciples went through between His crucifixion and Resurrection.

Imagine what it would have been like to be one of Jesus' disciples at the end. They watched as He was arrested, beaten, and crucified. All their hopes and dreams were rooted in Him, and then He was dead and seemingly defeated.

1

The confusion, hurt, and pain from that alone were probably unbearable, but then came the thoughts: *We have made such sacrifices, leaving family and businesses, risking it all on the belief that Jesus was the Messiah. Might it all have been in vain? How long before they come to get us?* That is real stress and pressure!

In this booklet, we're going to look at how Jesus prepared His own disciples for what they were about to go through between His death and Resurrection—and beyond! Just imagine if you had only one opportunity left to share everything you knew with the people who were closest to you. That's what Jesus did, and He knew it would be for their benefit—and ours! Think of it as a first-aid kit for any crisis you may face in your life.

Again, I'm not denying you have real problems, but you just need to see them in the light of what Jesus has already done and what He has already provided. Maybe it's a negative doctor's report, a financial debt, or a problem in your marriage. There's nothing too big for God! Praise the Lord!

'Don't You Dare Die!'

Years ago, I led a friend into the baptism of the Holy Spirit when he was in his 60s, and it radically transformed his life. It was a powerful experience, and he just fell in love with the Lord. But not long after that, he was diagnosed with cancer.

I tried sharing with this man about how to believe God for healing, but it was like he didn't care whether he got healed or not. He was just so in love with the Lord that going to be with Jesus didn't seem so bad to him—he was just ready to go. So, over time, the cancer got worse.

This man and his wife went on a vacation, but things got so bad they had to admit him to the hospital. The doctors said he wouldn't live through the night, but he just kept surviving. So, they rented an ambulance to take him home. His wife called to tell me about the situation, so I had her put the phone up to her husband's ear—because he was so weak—and I said, "Don't you dare die until I get there!"

I went over to this man's house and started ministering to him to build his faith. Over the next few months, I went to his house on nearly a daily basis, and I would pump him full of the Word of God. This man's health started to improve, and he got to where he was up and walking around. He was even driving his car!

It was miraculous the way this man began to recover as I ministered to him. I wasn't teaching him a specific passage of scripture. I was just sharing the things I had learned over decades of serving the Lord. And they were things you would tell people in a crisis situation.

His wife came to me one day and said, "The things that you're sharing with him have just transformed his life. It's obvious to see the way the Word is impacting him. You need to take these things, put them into a teaching and call it the *Christian Survival Kit*." (Years later, I ended up teaching an abbreviated version, which I called the *Christian First-Aid Kit*.)

As I prayed, I began to see the benefit of teaching what I had shared with my friend to others. But I asked the Lord, "Where would I teach this from? How do I take all these things that I've learned about what to do in a crisis situation and find them in the Word?"

'Let Not Your Heart Be Troubled'

Simon Peter said unto him, Lord, whither goest thou? Jesus answered him, Whither I go, thou canst not follow me now; but thou shalt follow me afterwards. Peter said unto him, Lord, why cannot I follow thee now? I will lay down my life for thy sake. Jesus answered him, Wilt thou lay down thy life for my sake? Verily, verily, I say unto thee, The cock shall not crow, till thou hast denied me thrice.

John 13:36–38

At about that time, I was reading through the Bible, and I came across John 14-16. That's where Jesus, the night before his crucifixion, was speaking with His disciples. It's one of the most detailed teachings of Jesus recorded in the Word. In those chapters, Jesus was teaching His disciples to prepare them for His crucifixion and the three days until the Resurrection. During that time, the disciples' faith was going to be tested to the max.

I know some of you think you're in a crisis right now. I'm not trying to belittle your situation, but if you look at your life from a historical perspective, it's nothing compared to what Jesus' disciples went through.

Jesus was preparing to leave, and He was turning His entire ministry over to His disciples. They were the ones Jesus was counting on to establish His church. So, I believe the demonic oppression going against them was greater than anything you and I have ever gone through.

The disciples had already given up their families for Jesus. They left their wives and children. They left their businesses. These people had given up everything. And for three and a half years, they followed Him.

Their hopes were so high on Jesus being the Messiah, that when He told them He would be crucified and then resurrected the third day, they just didn't understand. They weren't looking at their situation in the light of everything they saw Jesus do during that time, and realizing He would come out of the grave.

When they saw Jesus crucified, to them, it looked like He had lost! Their whole belief system was challenged. To them, it probably looked like everything Jesus prophesied hadn't come to pass. They were just crushed emotionally. It was a terrible situation!

I believe what the disciples went through was worse than anything any person reading this has gone through or ever will go through. Again, that's not to minimize the fact that you may have problems. It's just to say that this was a crisis situation of biblical proportions.

Harness Your Emotions

Let not your heart be troubled: ye believe in God, believe also in me.

John 14:1

Jesus had just shared with the disciples everything that would happen to Him, and He told Peter he would deny the Lord three times before the rooster crowed in the morning. But despite all that, Jesus told Peter and all the disciples not to let their hearts be troubled.

The understood subject of this verse is "you." It's up to you to control your heart. It's God's power that makes things possible, but we must make the choice and draw on God's ability. How do we do that? This verse goes on to say, "*believe also in me.*" Faith is how we conquer our emotions.

Even in circumstances like the disciples would experience, Jesus told them not to let their hearts be troubled. That's amazing! And it reveals the authority we have over our emotions. The Lord would have been unjust to command His disciples to do something they were powerless to do. Therefore, we can control our emotions regardless of how things are going.

The fact that Jesus mentions controlling our emotions first is also significant. If we let our emotions run away with us, then—as with a horse—it's nearly impossible to reign them in. It's easier to hold them at bay than it is to stop them once we have let them go. Harnessing your emotions is the first thing to do in a crisis situation. Most battles are won or lost in the first few moments, according to the way we allow our emotions to go.

The word *harness* means "to bring under control and direct the force of."[1] I believe this describes the way the Lord would have us deal with our emotions. He wants us to harness—to control and direct the force of—our emotions.

God created us with emotions to be enjoyed. Emotions are part of our soul. When God created the world, He looked at everything He made and said, "*Behold, it was very good*" (Gen. 1:31). So, emotions were created to be good things. I believe that emotions are one of the spices of life that make it worth living.

At the same time, many people find that their emotions are out of control. Emotions can be the very thing that drives people to depression, which causes all kinds of problems: divorce, anger, bitterness, hurt feelings, and even suicide. Emotions can actually control people.

I am not trying to condemn anyone, but I am saying that before you can experience victory, you must believe you have authority over your emotions. You don't have to be like an animal that just responds to everything by instinct. You have the power of choice (Deut. 30:19). You have authority over your emotions through Jesus Christ. You can walk in that authority and take control of your feelings.

The Issues of Life

Keep thy heart with all diligence; for out of it are *the issues of life.*

Proverbs 4:23

Your heart is the core of who you are, and it's where your spirit and soul—mind, will, emotions, and conscience—reside. This scripture tells us that we have the responsibility of keeping—or protecting—our hearts. You must be diligent in protecting your heart because the issues of life proceed out of it. In other words, your life actually comes out of your heart. So, it's up to you to not let your own heart be troubled.

The born-again spirit you receive at salvation already has the same life, nature, and ability of God in it (2 Cor. 5:17–18). What the apostle Paul says about the fruit of the Spirit (Gal. 5:22-23) is also true of the fruit of the born-again spirit. That spirit produces love, joy, peace, longsuffering, gentleness, goodness, faith, meekness, and temperance.

That means faith is a product of the spirit. Doubt and fear are the opposite of faith. Your born-again spirit doesn't operate in fear, but your heart can produce it along with doubt (Mark 11:23) and unbelief (Heb. 3:12).

Remember the Y2K scare at the turn of the millennium? It's a long story, but some people predicted that on January 1, 2000, computer systems around the world—and everything tied to them—would crash, causing widespread chaos.[2] Sad to say, many Christians believed it.

Churches sold generators and six-month supplies of emergency food. They urged people to move out of the cities. Many people proclaimed it would be the beginning of the Tribulation period.

The Lord had already told me to go on television and my program wasn't scheduled to broadcast until January 3, 2000. So, if everything that was predicted to happen actually occurred, then I wouldn't be on television! Based on that, I believed Y2K wouldn't result in disaster. And, wouldn't you know, it turned out to be a nonevent!

The world likes to exaggerate, lie, and present people with potential worst-case scenarios because bad news sells. Instead of the nightly news, it's become more like the nightly prophecy! This seemed to be the case during the pandemic response in 2020. People bought into all the bad news and made corresponding decisions contrary to the Word of God.

Those kinds of responses don't come out of a born-again spirit, which doesn't produce fear. They come from the soulish part of the heart that was programmed according to a person's sin nature before they were born again. That's why it's important for you to renew your mind—or reprogram it—according to God's promises in His Word!

Raising-from-the-Dead Power

Jesus said the key to not letting your heart be troubled is to believe. You've got to recognize that there is a God part on the inside of you. If you've been born again, you are the one who is supposed to be overcoming the world instead of the world overcoming you.

You have the same power on the inside of you that raised Jesus Christ from the dead (Rom. 8:11). That means you should react differently than a person who doesn't have God on the inside of them. You need to stand up and say, "I am not going to let this situation trouble me. I am not going to lose my faith."

Maybe you've let yourself get into discouragement and unbelief. I am not condemning you, but I am saying that you don't have to stay there. You don't have to live that way. But, sad to say, most people would rather have you put your arm around them, give them a hug, say, "We're praying for you," and just cry with them. They would rather have that than have somebody tell them the truth and set them free.

I am not trying to be insensitive to people. I believe you can have compassion, but if you are so empathetic that you get into the same pain and grief as somebody else, then you will become useless to them. As a matter of fact, it's because I love people that I teach that we are not just mere human beings. If you are born again, you have raising-from-the-dead power living on the inside of you. *AMEN*

The world wants you to believe that you can't overcome sickness, heartache, or any problem you face. The world wants you to think, *If somebody divorces you, you ought to be absolutely devastated. If your children die, you ought to just grieve the rest of your life. You ought to never be the same.* Some people actually fight for the right to be hurt, to live in pain, and just limp through life because of their problems.

I remember when I got the call telling us that our youngest son had died. I started experiencing all the negative emotions a person would feel in that moment. But I realized my response was critical. So, I said, "Well, the first report is not the last report!" As my wife, Jamie, and I were driving to the hospital, we just began praising the Lord and thanking Him for all the good things He'd already done.

I remember looking over at Jamie and telling her, "This is going to be the greatest miracle we have ever seen!"

When we arrived at the hospital, our oldest son met us at the door and said, "I don't know what happened, but right after I got off the phone with you, they said he sat up and started talking." Praise the Lord! AMEN

You Are Heaven Bound

In my Father's house are many mansions: if it were not so, I would have told you. I go to prepare a place for you. And if I go and prepare a place for you, I will come again, and receive you unto myself; that where I am, there *ye may be also.*

John 14:2–3

It's also important to keep your problems in perspective. Jesus began by telling His disciples not to let their hearts be troubled as they were about to enter the worst crisis of their lives. In the following verse, He began to speak about heaven. What does heaven have to do with us keeping our hearts at peace?

Well, even if everything in this life looks terrible, Christians always have the promises of total victory in heaven. No matter what situation you're in, you can always close your eyes and think about your great reward in heaven. That will keep your heart from being troubled.

Years ago, I took a trip to China where I met people in the underground church who had been beaten and tortured for their faith. One man had been imprisoned for ten years. He endured unspeakable things, yet he never denied his faith.

By the time I met this man, he had been out of prison for twenty years. Over that period, he started over 200,000 small home churches. More than 10 million people have been reached with the Gospel because of his commitment.

For security reasons, most people in his churches don't know who he is. He has very little money, and the world will likely never know about his sacrifice. I can't even tell you his name because his government is probably still looking for him. When you look at people like that, it makes the problems we face here in the West pale in comparison.

I'm sure this man had plenty of opportunities to let his heart be troubled, and yet he persevered. People in those kinds of situations can look at the reward of heaven and just see beyond whatever hardship they are going through at that moment.

I once had someone in our Bible school come to me with a complaint—and this person always seemed to have something to complain about! This time, he was crying about how he had been in a church service and was trying to listen to the message, but two ladies sat in front of him and talked the whole time. So, this person was upset because "Satan stole the Word" from him. My only question was, "Why didn't you just get up and move?"

In contrast, I had just gotten off the phone with a friend whose wife had gone on to be with the Lord. I was calling to check on him, but instead of crying about how bad things were, he was just rejoicing in the Lord. He was thanking God for His goodness and told me that the Holy Spirit was comforting him. He was not letting his heart be troubled.

This Is a Light Affliction

For our light affliction, which is but for a moment, worketh for us a far more exceeding and *eternal weight of glory.*

2 Corinthians 4:17

Whatever problems we face in this life will fade when we consider them in the light of eternity and what awaits us as born-again believers. That's the reason why the apostle Paul could call his afflictions "*light*."

It certainly wasn't because he didn't have any problems. In 2 Corinthians 11:23–30, Paul lists some of his light afflictions. He was beaten with rods and whips multiple times, stoned, left for dead, imprisoned, and shipwrecked. He suffered hunger, cold, and nakedness. He went through all this for the sake of the Gospel.

Paul probably suffered more than anyone reading this. And yet, his afflictions were only "light."

How did he take the heavy problems he encountered and turn them into just light afflictions? It was all in his focus. The way we think makes our problems big or small. Paul did three things that diminished his sufferings.

First, Paul knew all his suffering in this life was only like a moment in comparison to eternity. That puts everything in perspective. Those who are crumbling under their heavy loads are always shortsighted. They have become consumed with what is happening to them at that moment and forget that bad things don't last forever. Everything in this life is only temporary.

One of my favorite scriptures is, "It came to pass" (Matt. 11:1). That's why something comes—so it can pass! The sun will still come up tomorrow. And even if we find ourselves in a situation that may last a lifetime, that's only temporary too. We will live much longer in the blessings of heaven than in the hardships of earth.

Second, Paul knew that all his suffering would work out to his eternal benefit. We have great things awaiting us in glory. Jesus endured the cross by focusing on "*the joy that was set before him*" (Heb. 12:2).

The night before they entered their greatest trials, Jesus told His disciples about the mansions He would prepare for them (John 14:2–3). He did this to get their attention focused on the prize instead of the effort put forth to obtain the prize. Comparing our hardships here to the benefit awaiting us will always tip the scale in favor of the positive. As Paul said in Romans 8:18,

> *For I reckon that the sufferings of this present time* are *not worthy* to be compared *with the glory which shall be revealed in us.*

Third, Paul focused his attention on the permanent things of the spiritual realm instead of the temporary things of this physical world.

Look at Eternal Things

While we look not at the things which are seen, but at the things which are not seen: for the things which are seen are *temporal; but the things which* are *not seen* are *eternal.*

2 Corinthians 4:18

Paul wasn't saying he was ignorant of the problems in this life or in denial of their existence. He just didn't focus on the physical, temporary things of this world. He was more focused on the eternal, intangible things of the spiritual realm.

This is a key. We can never be truly effective if we are focused on this physical life only. Carnal life is terminal. If all we think about is this physical life, we have reason for sadness and cynicism (1 Cor. 15:19).

Life can be hard. But when we factor in eternity and all the wonderful things God has awaiting us, this physical life becomes a steppingstone to something awesome! This knowledge must permeate everything we think and do.

Most of us take the little things that Satan puts in our lives—all the problems that come our way—and we magnify them. It's like we take a tiny little pebble and turn it into a huge boulder. You see, your mind is like a pair of binoculars, which can either magnify or decrease something, depending on how you use them.

If you came to our Charis campus in Colorado, you would see Pikes Peak right outside the window. If you looked through a pair of binoculars, they would make Pikes Peak look huge and up close. You could see all kinds of details on the mountain. But you could take that exact same set of binoculars, turn them around, and you could shrink Pikes Peak so it looks tiny and far away. You can use your mind like a pair of binoculars.

For example, if the doctor says you've got cancer and you're going to die, you can start magnifying that, or you can take the promises of God and magnify them. You can say, "I believe I'm going to see God's healing power manifest in my life, and this is going to work out for His glory!"

You can use your mind to magnify something or reduce it in your sight.

Whatever you focus on gets bigger. If you focus on problems—like a bad report from your doctor or the amount of bills you have to pay—they will get bigger. Now, I'm not saying that you totally ignore problems. You need to confront situations and deal with them head on, but you need to deal with them in the light of God's promises. Rather than magnifying the temporary problems you're facing, look ahead to eternity.

You Know the Way

And whither I go ye know, and the way ye know. Thomas saith unto him, Lord, we know not whither thou goest; and how can we know the way?

John 14:4–5

Jesus was not asking a question. He was making a state-ment. Jesus said they knew where He was going and how to get there. However, Thomas contradicted Him, saying, *We don't know where You are going, and if we don't know that, how can we know the way to where You are going?*

21

Who was right, Jesus or Thomas? Jesus went on to explain that He was going to His Father and that He was the only way to approach the Father. "*I am the way, the truth, and the life,*" He said (John 14:6). Jesus had already explained these things to His disciples before; they just failed to make the connection. So, Jesus, of course, was the one who was correct. He always is.

When the Lord says we know something, we would be smart to just keep our mouths shut and not make fools of ourselves (Prov. 17:28). But Thomas opened his mouth and stuck his foot in it. There's a reason these guys were called *duh*-sciples!

That may be funny, but you can learn something from it. You may not understand something the Lord has said in His Word, but you should never take the position of contradicting it. It's alright to seek clarification or explanation (John 14:22), but you should never trust in your own understanding more than God's Word (Prov. 3:5).

Often, people cry out for God to speak to them while their Bibles are right there next to them on their nightstands. God has spoken to people through His Word. People just need to believe it and receive its truths as their way to victory.

What's more, Philip went on to say, "Show us the Father, and that will be enough" (John 14:8). You see, Philip wasn't completely satisfied with Jesus. Although he had witnessed Jesus perform miracles that no one had ever done before, speak as no one had ever spoken before, and love him as no one had ever loved him before, that wasn't enough. He wanted something more than Jesus before he would be satisfied.

It was because Philip only knew Jesus according to His flesh (2 Cor. 5:16). That is to say, Philip didn't know the real Jesus. He didn't fully recognize who Jesus was because of His physical body. Jesus' humanity hid His divinity from them.

Are You Satisfied?

Jesus saith unto him, Have I been so long time with you, and yet hast thou not known me, Philip? he that hath seen me hath seen the Father; and how sayest thou then, *Shew us the Father?*

John 14:9

Jesus was God manifest in the flesh (1 Tim. 3:16). He was the Lord God Almighty at His birth (Luke 2:11), but that glory was wrapped in the physical flesh of a tiny baby. His flesh was sinless, but it was still flesh. Isaiah said that there was no beauty in Jesus' flesh that He should be desired (Is. 53:2).

Jesus had to grow in His physical body and in His physical mind (Luke 2:52). His flesh looked as natural as any ordinary man. And because the true person of Jesus was veiled by His flesh, Philip and the other disciples didn't fully recognize who Jesus really was. They had the disadvantage of seeing Jesus' physical body.

Maybe you're thinking, *What do you mean "disadvantage"?* Many people think it would have been wonderful to see Jesus in the flesh, but it would also have made it harder to perceive who He really was.

I once had a dream where I was one of Jesus' disciples. It was so vivid, I thought it was real. I saw Him raise the dead and give sight to the blind. I was rejoicing with the other disciples over all the things we had seen and heard. Then Jesus turned around and challenged me by saying, "But who do you say I am?"

Although I had seen Him do things that no mortal man could do, when I looked straight into the face of His humanity, it took all the faith I could muster to say, "You are the Christ, the Son of the living God" (Matt. 16:15–16). I had to go beyond what I was seeing with my eyes, and I had to speak from my heart by faith (Rom. 10:10). Through that dream, I can somewhat imagine how hard it must have been for the disciples.

We have the advantage of seeing Jesus through the scriptures with the witness of the

Holy Spirit. Jesus' twelve disciples had to overcome His humanity every day. We don't. They only knew Jesus after the flesh. We can see Jesus with the eyes of our hearts through the revelation God has given us in Scripture. They couldn't do that, yet many Christians today have a similar problem believing what the Word of God says about healing, deliverance, prosperity, and all that Jesus has made available.

Perceive with Your Spirit

The vast majority of Christians today don't have spiritual perception. They may have the capacity for it, but they're just walking after the flesh, like the disciples. The Word of God is spirit, and it is life (John 6:63). It also says that you were healed by the stripes of Jesus (1 Pet. 2:24).

Some people will see that in their Bibles, but it doesn't matter. What's more important to them is what the doctor has to say or what their bodies are experiencing, and they just negate the power of the Word. They are being carnal-minded because they are going by what they feel. They make what they see, hear, smell, taste, and feel more important than what they believe.

But you can reverse this. You can get to a place where the Word of God dominates you more than physical, natural facts. You can get to where the Word is more real to you, and you'll know things by the spirit better than you know them by your mind.

Jesus told His disciples He was going to be crucified, and He told them He would rise from the dead. He was even specific enough to say that He would rise on the third day. But His Words didn't matter to them as much as what they had seen. They were walking by sight. Because of this, when Jesus rose from the dead, they couldn't recognize

Him. They were only operating in the natural. But we must perceive Jesus spiritually.

We can't know God in just physical terms. We must know God by and through the Spirit. God is a Spirit, and those who worship Him must worship Him in spirit and in truth (John 4:24). If the disciples had known Jesus in spirit, they would have longed for nothing more. He was every bit God. They just didn't fully realize who He was.

Philip was basically asking for the same thing that Moses asked for in Exodus 33:18–34:8 when Moses asked God to show him His glory. The difference was that Moses didn't have Jesus standing in front of him, and Philip did. Jesus is the express image of the Father (Heb. 1:3). There is no greater manifestation of God than what Jesus gave us.

And it's not the physical flesh of Jesus that revealed the express image of God. It was the actions and words of Jesus that revealed the true Christ (John 10:37-38). We can get that same revelation by seeing Jesus through the Word with the revelation knowledge of the Holy Spirit. We don't have to ask, nor do we need to see anything more than Jesus (John 20:29).

Do What Jesus Did

Verily, verily, I say unto you, He that believeth on me, the works that I do shall he do also; and greater works than these shall he do; because I go unto my Father.

John 14:12

People ask me about this verse nearly all the time. They typically want to know what the "greater works" are, and I'll ask them, "Are you already doing the works that Jesus did?" If they say, "No," then I'll tell them to just focus on the works that Jesus did—seeing people raised from the dead, blind eyes opened, deaf ears opened—and be satisfied with those before they start looking for the greater works.

Years ago, I preached on this verse at a meeting in Corpus Christi, Texas. The pastor of that church was so touched by what I ministered on that he fasted and prayed for a few days before the next Sunday service.

When he got up before his congregation, he said, "We are going to see miracles. We will see the dead raised. We are going to see blind eyes open," and on and on he went.

But while he was up there preaching, a man in the church stood up, grabbed his heart, and fell over dead!

A nurse in the congregation confirmed that the man was dead, and they called 911 for help. Even though the local fire department was across the street from the church, it ended up being twenty minutes before an ambulance arrived. While the people in the church were waiting, the pastor said, "Let's pray."

As the pastor was praying, it just dawned on him—*I've just been saying that we're going to see the dead raised.* So, he walked over to the dead man on the floor and said, "In the name of Jesus, get up!" And this guy just stood up. When the paramedics arrived and they took him to the hospital, they said, "You're perfect. There's nothing wrong with you." He was raised from the dead!

When you're in a crisis situation, you need to expect the supernatural. Really you need to start expecting before you get into a crisis. You need to start building yourself up right now, even if everything is going well. Meditate on scriptures about healing, prosperity, deliverance, and miracles.

I once took every scripture in the Bible where a person was raised from the dead, wrote them out on a piece of paper, and I just started meditating on them. That allowed the Word to become alive on the inside of me. I got to where I would dream every night of raising twenty to thirty people from the dead.

After a while, it just consumed me. Not long after seeing these things in my imagination, they moved from the spiritual into the natural. A man died in one of my services and we saw him raised from the dead. That's awesome!

The Spirit Is Your Comforter

And I will pray the Father, and he shall give you another Comforter, that he may abide with you for ever.

John 14:16

Notice that Jesus calls the Holy Spirit the "Comforter," not the afflicter. Scripture also says that He will send "another" Comforter. "Another" means one "of the same sort."[3] Jesus was and still is a comforter; He didn't condemn people during His earthly ministry.

Most people have been led to believe that self-doubt, self-condemnation, feelings of unworthiness, and conviction for individual sins are the work of the Holy Spirit. But it's just not true! The ministry of the Holy Spirit in the life of the believer is the front line of defense against the devil and his devices of defeat.

One of the ministries of the Holy Spirit is to bring back to our remembrance all things that Jesus has spoken to us. This is the best note-taking system available. Everything that Jesus speaks will be brought back to us. This is particularly valuable in a crisis situation.

The devil's favorite tool, religion, has done a great job of convincing the body of Christ that the Holy Spirit is the source of negative feelings. He has believers convinced it's the Holy Spirit showing them they are unworthy, and they must "clean up their acts" if they ever want to receive from the Lord.

The Holy Spirit doesn't convict people of things they do that are wrong, but of the fact that they aren't believing on Jesus (John 16:8–9). Those who don't tithe or give will not be convicted about their lack of giving, but about the fact that they aren't trusting Jesus with their finances. All acts of sin come from the one act of not believing on and resting in relationship with Jesus.

The reason not to steal is because that action reveals a lack of trust in God as our source. The real reason not to commit adultery is because that act reveals that we do not believe the Lord when He said that *"from the beginning . . . God made them male and female,"* and that the two are to become one flesh (Mark 10:6–8). People who commit adultery are just not content with the mate the Lord has given them, and they are showing that they are not full of God's love. If they were, they would not be looking to someone else to fill that void.

Hebrews 4:15 says that Jesus was tempted in all points like as we are, yet He was without sin. Jesus may not have been tempted with some of the things we face today, but He was tempted with unbelief. And that is the root of all sin. Jesus endured that temptation in all its facets.

The Gift of Tongues

One of the key benefits of having the Holy Spirit is receiving the gift of speaking in tongues. It is not only one of the first things that happens after being baptized in the Holy Spirit, but it's also one of the most important.

When you pray in tongues, it is your spirit that prays (1 Cor. 14:14). Your spirit is the part of you that is born again and has the mind of Christ (1 Cor. 2:16). So, in your spirit, you have unlimited knowledge, and all you have to do is draw it out. The Bible says that when you pray in tongues, your spirit, the part of you that has that knowledge, is praying.

If you pray in tongues, pray also for the interpretation (1 Cor. 14:13). I have prayed in the spirit many times when confronted with a crisis. In the natural, when I just don't have the ability or self-confidence to conquer something, I pray in tongues. I seek the Lord, and I don't lean on my own understanding.

When I run into a problem, I pray in tongues and ask God for wisdom. I also pray for God to give me the interpretation. If I'm praying and nobody else is around, I don't need to speak it out. I just need my understanding enlightened (Eph. 1:18). I could give you testimony after testimony about how this special communication with God has blessed me.

One of the most miraculous occurrences in my life and ministry was when we were waiting on a $3.2 million loan for a building project. The process was dragging out for so long that eventually the lender wanted us to start the whole process over. So, I said, "God, there's got to be an answer."

I started praying in tongues and asked Him what to do and for the interpretation. It was only a few minutes before the Lord reminded me of a prophecy that had come to me two years before. I hadn't denied it. I just hadn't remembered it.

The prophecy was that I didn't need a bank loan—my partners would finance whatever I needed. Fourteen months later we had $3.2 million. And all of that came from praying in tongues and praying for an interpretation.

Not realizing this truth is like dying of thirst while leaning against a well filled with water because you don't know how to draw it out. Speaking in tongues is drawing out the Holy Spirit. Then afterwards you pray to receive the interpretation from God. It's like a key that unlocks the power of God and builds you up so you can respond to any crisis.

Jesus Left Us Peace

Peace I leave with you, my peace I give unto you: not as the world giveth, give I unto you. Let not your heart be troubled, neither let it be afraid. Ye have heard how I said unto you, I go away, and come again unto you. If ye loved me, ye would rejoice, because I said, I go unto the Father: for my Father is greater than I.

John 14:27–28

What a powerful revelation! If Jesus' disciples had loved Him more than they loved themselves, they would have rejoiced at His death. How is that?

Jesus had suffered criticism and rejection in this world like no one else ever has. Jesus also spoke constantly of longing to go to His Father. So, if the disciples had only been thinking of Jesus, they could have actually rejoiced at His death, because at least Jesus would then be at peace and reunited with His Father.

But the disciples weren't thinking about the welfare of Jesus. They were selfish—they were thinking about themselves. They believed Jesus would establish His earthly kingdom and that they would rule with Him. They may have been thinking, *What will happen to us if Jesus is killed? What will we do? Where will we go?* Their sorrow was all about themselves.

Jesus was saying that if the disciples were thinking of Him more than they were thinking of themselves, they would be happy that Jesus was returning to the Father. This is always the case when believers die. There is no reason to sorrow for those who are gone; they are blessed beyond measure. Our sorrow is really for ourselves.

Years ago, the one-year-old daughter of one of our employees accidentally drowned in a pond. It was a tragic situation. The family didn't want a funeral, but they did have a viewing. So, I went, and many other people came to visit the family.

As I was standing there watching the other people, I heard them say many things that shed some light on the way they were thinking. They talked about how sad the situation was, but they also talked about how this child would never experience her first day of school, would never learn how to ride a bicycle, and on and on they went.

Over a hundred people showed up to this viewing, and they were just standing around and talking. So, the family came to me and asked if I would lead a memorial service right there, even though they hadn't planned on doing anything like that.

Don't Mourn for Yourself

I got up and started talking about what I'd been listening to other people say. I noted that they were talking about all the milestones this little girl would miss out on. Then I talked about all the negative things she wouldn't experience, like being picked on at school and having her heart broken. I also talked about how this girl went to be with the Lord, referencing when David's child died (2 Sam. 12:23).

I said that even though this was a tragic situation, this little girl was with Jesus. When they were talking about all the things they thought this girl would miss out on, they weren't really mourning for her—they were mourning for themselves. They were the ones who would miss out on all those things. People were sad, and understandably so, but that little girl was with the Lord.

People tend to not look at things that way because we've been trained by the world to think about all the bad things that could happen to us when a crisis hits. We focus on the situation from our point of view: *How can I go on without them? I won't ever see them again on earth.* We convince ourselves that we are mourning over the death of these people, but it's really over how it will affect us.

If that person is with Jesus, it should be a time to rejoice. Just imagine the atmosphere of a believer's funeral if we focused on the one who was with Jesus and what that person was experiencing rather than our own self-centered thoughts about what we are losing. Instead of grieving, what an exciting time of thanksgiving and praise it would be!

God created us to live our lives focused on Him. His purpose from the very beginning was that we should be "God-conscious," not "self-conscious." Until Adam and Eve ate the forbidden fruit from the Tree of Knowledge of Good and Evil, they were so unconscious of self that they did not even consider their own nakedness. But after their disobedience, they became fully aware of themselves and wanted to hide from God. Their focus had shifted from God to self.

Self-consciousness is just another way of saying self-centeredness, and self-centeredness really is the source of all grief. People grieve or are unhappy for many different reasons. But, if they analyze it, they would find that it is always the result of self being deprived of what it wants. So, the answer to dealing with grief can be found in dealing with self.

The correct way to deal with self is to shift your focus. Find someone who needs prayer or ministry. Help them in their situation, and you will find yourself forgetting about your own needs. But our ultimate focus has to be on God, not just others, and certainly not on ourselves. It's only when we are totally surrendered to God that we can love others.

Don't Get Offended

These things have I spoken unto you, that ye should not be offended.

John 16:1

Now, put this together with Jesus' teaching in Mark 4:14–17, where He talks about how the Sower sows the seed and Satan comes immediately to steal it away (v.

15). One of the things Satan uses to steal away the Word is afflictions and persecutions (v. 17). When that happens, people become offended.

When Jesus told His disciples, "I've spoken these words to you so that you would not be offended," what He's saying is, "I'm preparing you for a crisis situation, so that instead of you falling apart like a $2 suitcase, you will be able to stand and succeed."

We know from the Gospel accounts that all the disciples forsook Jesus and fled. They were in total disarray. They were discouraged and despondent. They didn't take hold of everything Jesus taught them in these chapters, but I believe He told them everything they needed to know so that they could survive a crisis situation and come through it without becoming depressed, discouraged, fearful, or offended.

Jesus prophesied multiple times about His Resurrection. He even made it very clear, comparing it to Jonas (Matt. 12:39-41), that it would be on the third day. So, He prepared them; He told them everything they needed to know. They could have survived and thrived through this. They could have actually looked through the eyes of faith and just thought, *This is exactly what Jesus told us. Everything is going according to plan.*

Even though they may not have rejoiced at seeing Jesus crucified, they could have rejoiced knowing that it was part of God's plan, that He was paying for their sins, and that it was part of the atonement. They could have walked in victory instead of defeat.

Jesus was preparing them, knowing that this was going to be a terrible situation. In the thirteenth chapter of John, right before He shared these things, Jesus—knowing everything that was going to happen unto Him—took His garments aside, wrapped Himself with a towel, and began to wash His disciples' feet. And the very last thing He did there was prophesy that Peter would betray Him three different times that very night (John 13:38).

That shows Jesus knew exactly what was coming, yet He took time to prepare His disciples. I believe He went back over three and a half years' worth of ministry and hit the highlights of what He had taught to prepare them. Jesus did this so that they would be able to stand and not waiver in between the crucifixion and Resurrection. Basically, He was preparing them for a major crisis situation.

Be of Good Cheer

These things I have spoken unto you, that in me ye might have peace. In the world ye shall have tribulation: but be of good cheer; I have overcome the world.

John 16:33

The Lord clearly stated that we will have trouble in this world, but we can still be of good cheer because He has overcome the world. There is no justification for us being defeated. God's provision is greater than all our needs.

Notice that our peace is dependent upon the words He has spoken to us. It's through God's Word that we renew our minds (Rom. 12:2). The Lord keeps us in perfect peace when our minds are stayed upon Him through taking heed to His Word (Is. 26:3).

I personally believe that people's first reactions to a crisis will dictate whether they overcome. Most people let their emotions and hurts run their course, giving them time to build huge strongholds of unbelief in their hearts. Then, after the strongholds have been well established, they turn to God and ask for help. They don't realize that it's much easier to keep the storm of a crisis from getting inside their hearts than it is to remove it later.

I think about the testimony of Alan and Debbie Moore. Debbie found Alan lying unresponsive on the ground. She called the ambulance, but she refused to panic. She was able to harness her emotions in the face of negative doctors' reports and stand in faith for Alan's healing from a massive stroke. She was so calm that the neurologist accused her of not taking him seriously.

"One-third of his brain is permanently damaged," said the doctors. "His left side is paralyzed. He'll never swallow or speak again, and he'll need a stomach tube for the rest of his life." Yet, just nine days later, Alan walked out of the hospital and returned to his job. A second MRI still showed "permanent" damage to Alan's brain, but he remained unaffected by the stroke. He was a walking miracle, and I believe he survived because Debbie understood that the first step is to not panic, and "let not your heart be troubled."

We live in a fallen world and tribulations will come. You cannot avoid them, but if you're prepared, you can keep them from getting on the inside of you. I don't care if you've been divorced, suffered financial disaster, or are facing cancer, God can turn your problem around if you will believe and not panic.

Keep Things in Perspective

One of the things that has struck me as I've traveled the world is how materialistic we are in America. Now, I'm not saying you should just give everything away and live in poverty, but you need to have some perspective. I praise God that I live in America, and I'm thankful for this nation and how God has prospered us as a people. But many people have skewed values.

Some people are bummed out because they aren't living in a million-dollar home. They think they're struggling because they don't own multiple cars and have five flat-screen televisions. In the light of eternity, these things just don't have any real significance.

I'm not against you if you own any of those things, and I am for prosperity, but it doesn't matter if you have gold jewelry, diamonds, or a home made of steel. It's all going to be destroyed! The most important things in life aren't things, and yet some people work two or three jobs trying to get more things they just don't need. They would be much better off to downsize, live within their means, and not have to be under all that pressure.

I've been out in the bush in Africa and seen people living in grass huts. I've been to India and seen whole houses that could fit inside just one bathroom in some of these large homes in the United States. Even if you are living in poverty in America, you're probably better off than people in China. And those people in the underground church who are being persecuted for their faith in Jesus are just happy and thrilled that they have it as good as they do. They have a perspective a lot of people in the American church just don't have!

When a person comes to the end of their life and is ready to die, nobody thinks, *I wish I would have bought a bigger house. I wish I would have driven a nicer car.* Instead, people say, "I wish I would have spent more time with my family," or "I wish I would have loved people more." One of the reasons people think they are in a crisis is because they don't think about their life in the light of eternity.

Sometimes I have to keep from laughing when people come forward for prayer at our meetings. They'll tell me what's going on and I think, *That's it? That's your big problem?* Often, things worse than that happen to me on my best days. I'm not denying that people have problems but, again, it's a matter of keeping things in perspective.

I've kept a journal for nearly twenty years, and I go back and read it every once in a while. It's amazing. I can't even remember some of the things that bothered me back then. They weren't important.

Rejoice in the Lord

Rejoice in the Lord alway: and *again I say, Rejoice.*
Philippians 4:4

My friend, Pastor Bob Nichols, has been a real encouragement to me. As a matter of fact, he's the one who gave me that statement, "The first report is not the last report." He pastored Calvary Cathedral in Fort Worth, Texas, for more than fifty years and still serves on the Board of Directors of our ministry.

As I've gotten to be good friends with Pastor Bob and his wife, Joy, I've watched them face some real crisis situations over the years. They have been through things that would have made someone else quit, but I've been really blessed by watching how they've responded.

Years ago, Pastor Bob's church building was destroyed by a tornado. Not long after that, he was on the internet confidently stating they were going to end up with a facility twice as nice as the one that was destroyed. He chose to believe God, have peace, and not panic.

That following Sunday, they held church elsewhere and some reporters showed up. I'm sure they expected everyone to be in tears. But they were shocked that people were actually positive and kept a good attitude—they didn't let their hearts be troubled.

I remember one year, at a ministers' conference, I was teaching on glorifying and praising God, and Pastor Bob was sitting there on the front row. Suddenly, he stood up, threw his Bible on the floor, and yelled, "I've had just about all of this I can stand!" That kind of shocked everybody and really got their attention. Then, he said, "I've just got to praise God for how good things already are!"

Now, at that time, Bob and Joy's daughter had some serious health problems. She had been in a coma. Although she came out of it and they saw progress, the family struggled under those conditions longer than most people would endure. But in the midst of it all, Pastor Bob still praised God.

He did this in a room full of ministers, and many of them knew what Pastor Bob and Joy had gone through. Wouldn't you know, it just ruined my whole sermon! People got to shouting and praising God and other people repented for griping and complaining. And it all happened because a man who had suffered more than most of us have ever even thought about suffering just decided to praise God for all the good things He'd already done. That's awesome!

Conclusion

We live in a fallen world, so you will face problems. You cannot keep problems from coming, but how you respond when a crisis hits is really important. You can keep those problems from getting on the inside of you. It's your choice whether you become bitter or better.

If you plan on serving God with your life, you are going to encounter some resistance. When you begin to fulfill your God-given purpose, Satan is going to fight you. There is a devil going around like a roaring lion, seeking whom he may devour (1 Pet. 5:8).

If you never bump into the devil in this life, it might be because you're going in the same direction. But when you turn around and begin following God's plan for your life, you're going to get some resistance, and you will need to know how to keep your heart from being troubled.

There are going to be crisis situations in your life, but they don't have to overwhelm you. You can keep the right perspective on life, rely on the Holy Spirit, be at peace, and keep praising God, no matter the circumstances.

Jesus told His disciples all these things so they would walk in victory and not be offended—and He is no respecter of persons! I believe that if you put the Word of God to work in your own life, you will experience God's very best, and you will overcome any crisis!

FURTHER STUDY

If you enjoyed this booklet and would like to learn more about some of the things I've shared, I suggest my teachings:

1. *Christian Survival Kit*
2. *How to Prepare Your Heart*
3. *Harness Your Emotions*
4. *As I Have Loved You*
5. *Are You Satisfied with Jesus?*

These teachings are available for free at **awmi.net**, or they can be purchased at **awmi.net/store**.

Receive Jesus as Your Savior

Choosing to receive Jesus Christ as your Lord and Savior is the most important decision you'll ever make!

God's Word promises, *"That if thou shalt confess with thy mouth the Lord Jesus, and shalt believe in thine heart that God hath raised him from the dead, thou shalt be saved. For with the heart man believeth unto righteousness; and with the mouth confession is made unto salvation"* (Rom. 10:9–10). *"For whosoever shall call upon the name of the Lord shall be saved"* (Rom. 10:13). By His grace, God has already done everything to provide salvation. Your part is simply to believe and receive.

Pray out loud: "Jesus, I acknowledge that I've sinned and need to receive what you did for the forgiveness of my sins. I confess that You are my Lord and Savior. I believe in my heart that God raised You from the dead. By faith in Your Word, I receive salvation now. Thank You for saving me."

The very moment you commit your life to Jesus Christ, the truth of His Word instantly comes to pass in your spirit. Now that you're born again, there's a brand-new you!

Please contact us and let us know that you've prayed to receive Jesus as your Savior. We'd like to send you some free materials to help you on your new journey. Call our Helpline: **719-635-1111** (available 24 hours a day, seven days a week) to speak to a staff member who is here to help you understand and grow in your new relationship with the Lord.

Welcome to your new life!

Receive the Holy Spirit

As His child, your loving heavenly Father wants to give you the supernatural power you need to live a new life. *"For every one that asketh receiveth; and he that seeketh findeth; and to him that knocketh it shall be opened...how much more shall your heavenly Father give the Holy Spirit to them that ask him?"* (Luke 11:10–13).

All you have to do is ask, believe, and receive! Pray this: "Father, I recognize my need for Your power to live a new life. Please fill me with Your Holy Spirit. By faith, I receive it right now. Thank You for baptizing me. Holy Spirit, You are welcome in my life."

Some syllables from a language you don't recognize will rise up from your heart to your mouth (1 Cor. 14:14). As you speak them out loud by faith, you're releasing

God's power from within and building yourself up in the spirit (1 Cor. 14:4). You can do this whenever and wherever you like.

It doesn't really matter whether you felt anything or not when you prayed to receive the Lord and His Spirit. If you believed in your heart that you received, then God's Word promises you did. *"Therefore I say unto you, What things soever ye desire, when ye pray, believe that ye receive* them, *and ye shall have* them" (Mark 11:24). God always honors His Word—believe it!

We would like to rejoice with you, pray with you, and answer any questions to help you understand more fully what has taken place in your life!

Please contact us to let us know that you've prayed to be filled with the Holy Spirit and to request the book *The New You & the Holy Spirit*. This book will explain in more detail about the benefits of being filled with the Holy Spirit and speaking in tongues. Call our Helpline: **719-635-1111** (available 24 hours a day, seven days a week).

Endnotes

1. *American Heritage Dictionary*, s.v. "harness," accessed November 7, 2023, https://ahdictionary.com/word/search.html?q=harness

2. "Y2K," National Museum of American History, accessed October 27, 2023, https://americanhistory.si.edu/collections/object-groups/y2k

3. *Vine's Expository Dictionary of New Testament Words*, s.v. "another," accessed November 15, 2023, https://www.blueletterbible.org/search/Dictionary/viewTopic.cfm?topic=VT0000126

Call for Prayer

If you need prayer for any reason, you can call our Helpline, 24 hours a day, seven days a week at **719-635-1111**. A trained prayer minister will answer your call and pray with you.

Every day, we receive testimonies of healings and other miracles from our Helpline, and we are ministering God's nearly-too-good-to-be-true message of the Gospel to more people than ever. So, I encourage you to call today!

About the Author

Andrew Wommack's life was forever changed the moment he encountered the supernatural love of God on March 23, 1968. As a renowned Bible teacher and author, Andrew has made it his mission to change the way the world sees God.

Andrew's vision is to go as far and deep with the Gospel as possible. His message goes far through the *Gospel Truth* television program, which is available to over half the world's population. The message goes deep through discipleship at Charis Bible College, headquartered in Woodland Park, Colorado. Founded in 1994, Charis has campuses across the United States and around the globe.

Andrew also has an extensive library of teaching materials in print, audio, and video. More than 200,000 hours of free teachings can be accessed at **awmi.net**.

Contact Information

Andrew Wommack Ministries, Inc.

PO Box 3333
Colorado Springs, CO 80934-3333
info@awmi.net
awmi.net

Helpline: 719-635-1111 (available 24/7)

Charis Bible College

info@charisbiblecollege.org
844-360-9577
CharisBibleCollege.org

For a complete list of all of our offices,
visit **awmi.net/contact-us**.

Connect with us on social media.

Andrew's LIVING COMMENTARY BIBLE SOFTWARE

Andrew Wommack's *Living Commentary* Bible study software is a user-friendly, downloadable program. It's like reading the Bible with Andrew at your side, sharing his revelation with you verse by verse.

Main features:
- Bible study software with a grace-and-faith perspective
- Over 26,000 notes by Andrew on verses from Genesis through Revelation
- *Matthew Henry's Concise Commentary*
- 12 Bible versions
- 2 concordances: *Englishman's Concordance* and *Strong's Concordance*
- 2 dictionaries: *Collaborative International Dictionary* and *Holman's Dictionary*
- Atlas with biblical maps
- Bible and *Living Commentary* statistics
- Quick navigation, including history of verses
- Robust search capabilities (for the Bible and Andrew's notes)
- "Living" (i.e., constantly updated and expanding)
- Ability to create personal notes

Whether you're new to studying the Bible or a seasoned Bible scholar, you'll gain a deeper revelation of the Word from a grace-and-faith perspective.

Purchase Andrew's *Living Commentary* today at **awmi.net/living**, and grow in the Word with Andrew.

Item code: 8350

ANDREW WOMMACK MINISTRIES